DANCE WITH A SHADOW

Irina Ratushinskaya

TRANSLATED BY
David McDuff

BLOODAXE BOOKS

ISBN: 1 85224 232 9 hardback edition
       1 85224 233 7 paperback edition

First published 1992 by
Bloodaxe Books Ltd,
P.O. Box 1SN,
Newcastle upon Tyne NE99 1SN.

Bloodaxe Books Ltd acknowledges
the financial assistance of Northern Arts.

Cover printing by J. Thomson Colour Printers Ltd, Glasgow.

Printed in Great Britain by
Cromwell Press Ltd, Broughton Gifford, Melksham, Wiltshire.

Acknowledgements

Most of these poems are translated from Irina Ratushinskaya's collected volume *Stikhi* (Literaturnyi kur'er, Chicago, 1988). The poems in the last section of the book are translations from uncollected work.

Contents

PUBLISHER'S NOTE

Irina Ratushinskaya was arrested on 17 September 1982 and held in the KGB Prison in Kiev. She was only 28-years-old when she was sentenced to seven years' hard labour and five years' internal exile, accused of anti-Soviet agitation and propaganda. Her crime: writing poetry.

The poems which a Soviet judge had called 'a danger to the State' were published by Bloodaxe in her book *No, I'm Not Afraid* in 1986. She herself was unaware that they had been smuggled out, and that an international campaign was being mounted on her behalf, spear-headed by a book of her own poetry.

In a "strict regime" labour camp at Barashevo in Mordovia, she was held for three years in the Small Zone, a special unit for women political prisoners. There she suffered beatings, force-feeding and solitary confinement in brutal, freezing conditions, and became so ill that many feared she would not survive her sentence. The KGB told her she would never be able to bear children.

In the camp Irina wrote poems with burnt matchsticks onto bars of soap, and then memorised them. Later she would copy them in a tiny hand onto strips of paper which were hidden and smuggled out of the camp. She first heard that her poems had been published around the world when the KGB came to see her in the labour camp. They told her she would get another ten years for having her work published in the West.

The rest is history. Mikhail Gorbachev and Ronald Reagan were given copies of her book. On 9 October 1986, on the eve of the Reykjavik summit, Irina Ratushinskaya was released, after serving four years of her sentence. She was allowed to leave Russia in December 1986 to come to Britain for urgent medical treatment, and after living in America for a year, she settled in London with her husband Igor Geraschenko. Since coming to the West she has been treated by doctors for the injuries and illnesses she contracted in prison. Finally, in February 1992, she gave birth to twin sons, Sergei and Oleg.

As well as the book which helped bring about her release, *No, I'm Not Afraid*, she published a second collection, *Pencil Letter* (Bloodaxe Books, 1988), and two volumes of autobiography with Hodder, *Grey Is the Colour of Hope* (1988), about her time in the labour camp, and *In the Beginning* (1990), which tells the story of her childhood, education and marriage to a dissident, her beliefs and Christian faith, and her persecution by the KGB. Irina has nearly always dated her poems, and noted the place of composition, so they can be related to the poems in her other two Bloodaxe collections and to the events in her life described in her two autobiographical memoirs.

In the labour camp she mostly lived in the Small Zone, the compound for women political prisoners, but was also locked up for long periods in a punishment isolation cell, or SHIZO (*shtrafnoy izolyator*), and at other times in the camp's internal prison, or PKT (*Pomescheniye Kamernogo Tipa*), at Yavas. These initials are used in this book to indicate where, and under what conditions, particular poems were written. The camp itself had no name, but was identified as ZhKh–385, and the different numbers following this (2 or 3-4) relate to particular parts of the sprawling network of prison camps near Barashevo, three hundred miles south-east of Moscow.

ODESSA 1970 – TASHKENT 1978

1.

Under vaults of cathedrals eternal,
Barefoot where dusty roads wind,
With nakedly trembling candles
People seek a God who is kind.

That He'll understand and take pity
Through the murders, the raving and lies,
That He'll put his hands on temples
As on cruel injuries.

That He'll see the shouting faces,
Dark of souls, eyes that light never knew,
That the fool and the whore He will pardon,
And the priest, and the poet, too.

That He'll save the fleer from pursuers,
That He'll give to the hungry bread...
Perhaps God is a cross in a hand's palm?
Perhaps God is a sky dark as lead?

The road to Him, how discover?
With what measure the hope, pain and grief?
People seek God, a kind one.
God grant they may find and believe.

Odessa, 1970

2.

Song of the Cat Who Walks Alone

A grey, sad rain is falling,
And I sit on a chimney alone.
In the porch someone's waiting for someone,
But I am all on my own.

A chain of tracks stretches behind me,
From my whiskers the water's a-flow,
But the rain will keep up until morning,
And perhaps for ever more.

Through the mist the trees will show blackly,
Their hands raised up in a plea.
But over the roofs I shall wander –
Again all on my own I'll be.

From the cruel and the kind I shall wander
And, like now, the rain will pour.
I know human beings – won't enter
When they throw wide-open the door.

They will want to stroke me,
Let me walk on their carpeted floors,
But what if they drown my kittens –
Wishing me well, of course.

And again someone's guilt will be lying
On the fate that is mine alone.
And over the roofs I shall wander –
Once again
            all on my own.

Odessa, 1971

3.

My fortune is a cheerful one –
She forgives my faithlessness
And with a haughty movement
I sweep the counters from the table.

And, perhaps, she is kind –
She knows how to laugh
The way clowns do
Getting up from the dusty carpet.

And how many times her wings
have traced the evening above me,
And in order to join hand with hand –
Me with you –
She has thrown from her wing
A golden ring,
But I have not taken the gift.

Odessa, 1976

4.

How random our meetings are!
The candle's shoulders are burning down,
The candle's fingers are melting.
Our thoughts are now afar –
And our poor evening has melted away,
Like the Snow Maiden on the stove.

Night stands at the window – barefoot.
We are pale, saving each other,
Warding off disaster with ourselves.
Covering the light with our hands,
We play the game
That I am not going now.

The years spent together,
The sadnesses and the the spells of bad weather
That have been sent down to us two,
That of which we shall both dream,
That which will never come true –
Is burning down,
And we are silent.

In a moment it will have burnt out –
And we'll get up,
And look each other in the eyes
Through the oncoming night:
And in the end we'll join hands,
And the silence – a sign of parting –
Spreading, will die in flight.

And there will be no other portents,
Only from the sea through the autumn mist
A long bell will go sounding.
Silent, our shadows will flit.
The candle's knees are burning down.
The candle's fingers are melting.

Odessa, 1977

5.

On my stove
No cricket sings.
In my night
There is only a scrap of light.
On my shoulder
No weeping spends the night.
On my candle
The tongue is hot!
From the light it has shone
There is no sadness for me...
The turn of a key.
In an hour it will be dawn.

6.

Well, take the guitar, then,
Take it onto your knee –
Like a child –
And touch the strings.
And bend your cheek to the wood,
And grip the neck like a spear –
With your whole hand.
From God are all other things.

In a few days' time
I will forget the tune and the words
And go
into a summer that's insane.
Like a wave it will grip my knees –
And the seaweed
Will muddle up
Evening and dawn again.

And then –
Snow upon snow –
Ever denser and denser
Will fly
Onto the disgraced roofs.
And for hundreds of unneeded earths
And lost days
Will I really
Not hear you?

With your telegram
I'll cross on the way, come flying –
And for a moment
I'll choke in the door...
Well, then, take the guitar,
Tune it –
And linger a little.
Before the long journey
Let's say no more.

Odessa, 1977

18

7.

Who's given it, to understand goodbyes –
The sundering of station shores?
Who can know why in the nights
The despair of silence lies
On the white guard of the snows?
Why is love the name they chose?
No name at all would be more wise.

Odessa, 1978

8.

This strange Thursday was born to be king,
But put on a jester's clothes.
And his reign began with rain
And the four winds in a row.
And in the wet streets it was dark
And along the high roads fire swept,
But the morning had been revoked –
And no one asked about it.

And a clown-play of unexpected meetings began,
And the lamps blazed like anything,
And the cloak was torn from the king's back
By the draughts from each theatre wing.
And suddenly we forgot our words –
And no one came to our aid.
In the prompter's box there sat an owl
And looked right through us, instead.

While Thursday, laughing, jingled his bell
And played the fool, out of place.
'A happy ending is easy,' he cried,
'But try one that's worked out by guess!
The plot wouldn't let you burn your boats,
So I've royally turned it down flat.
Today I command you to play without roles –
By God's mercy, Thursday – that's that!'

And then up we went onto the boards,
And stood there – hand in hand –
And they lay in the dust, by the sky not required,
The stage-property clouds.
And despair instead of words we had,
And our scripts were clean paper sheets.
We ignored the whistles from the gallery,
And the silence from the front seats.

And Thursday looked, and then went away –
No one noticed when.
And Friday, young and beautiful,
Did next the throne ascend.

Tashkent, 1978

KIEV 1979-82

9.

We'll go away to the land of Italy,
And from there somewhere else as well.
We'll take a little bell with us,
A couple of brushes and a notebook.
And there will be no righteous sacrifice for us,
No sentence
And acquittal.
There will only remain grounds
for those who know how to accuse.

You and I will buy a dog,
A big black one.
You'll build me a house of gingerbreads
With a small white tower and a window.
I'll forget how to cry in a whisper,
And I'll write you a letter,
The one that was intercepted
and filed away a long, long time ago.

And like children after an illness –
A new voice and a new gaze,
And now never lookng back,
We shall come to love other songs.
Let them accuse or not accuse.

Kiev, 1979

10.

The seventies are miserable!
The seventies have swallowed
So much shame!
Not even the board –
        of my coffin –
Will protect me
From the sweepings
        of those shameful years.
They'll take what's theirs – no more!
To some they'll slip a Party card,
To some – a passport and a savings book,
To some – a mental hospital,
        and to some –
Love that was born in captivity.
The unfed infant in your house,
Thrown out into the fields,
Will grow quiet by evening:
Not a cry,
Not a wheeze...
All's quiet. The
Seventies are a butcher!
Seventies not waiting
For the weather: neither by the seas*
(To go to the seas is forbidden!),
        nor by the fence...
Let there be a speedy end
To years which, wise
As reptiles, as snakes –
        come into every house,
And between every two – with bad weather!
A soul, born a slave!
An infant kicked out of the creche
For dis-loy-al-ty!
Throw the seventies the bone
Of the bone,
Leaving the flesh,
Into the eighties (Lord,
Preserve!) – almost weightless –
Go!

Already the dream is not frightening:
Go!
How the grass prickles...
Go!
Don't touch
The dug trench with a bare foot:
Suppose something were to rise up?
                    Cover you –
With a sheet?
What lies ahead there – do you know?
Don't ask!
If you're alive – go!

Kiev, 1979

*by the seas: in Russian, the expression *zhdat' u morya pogody* (literally: 'to wait for the weather by the sea') means 'to wait in vain for something'.

11.

We are a trick of laughing nature,
For whom to live to ripeness is disgrace,
For whom the wrinkles' careful pattern
Multiplies the shame of living all those days –
Oh, how we thirst for honour and the sword!
They are not given to us.
Removed before our birth
Not only sound of words but also their import,
And their enactment – and only speechlessness!
And only pain.
May it be short.

Kiev, 1979

12.

You and I will bring a Christmas tree – gauche little shy mite,
And with fright it will shake as you hold it aloft in your hands.
Long known to me, Christmas fear that a child understands –
A fire that is glazed, and the frost, so one can't get a word out!

On its timid small paw an amberstone ring I will lay,
And instead of a toy I will hang on a paper-chain quickly,
And then you will ruffle your palm through its summit so prickly,
And, courteous your bow, 'Happy January', you will say.

Happy January, our green little child. Don't look, never mind
That there's no white tablecloth and the walls are of others' giving.
Happy January, happy January! That means – December's behind,
The twenty-fifth revolt is behind, and still we're living!

Don't shake, little fool, our December's out stealing a horse.
Don't look – it's just the blind the wind's making billow...
For our tale we'll think up a happy ending, of course –
And believe in it for today. But not quickly tomorrow.

Kiev
1 January 1980

13.

Oh, how we knew how to to love: livened up by fingers!
Oh how aloofly near morning we were able to weep!
Now we understand it all,
                              but how we are tired.
Oh, how we grew tired towards midday,
                              covered in dust our feet.
And there were forks –
But the words on the signs were wiped away like a mirage,
And there were sadnesses –
But we continue to walk.
The sun pulsates,
                    and the throat that tastes of blood
Cannot produce a sound,
And a trembling erodes the ways.
But we already know when the prophecy will come true,
And what birds, black
                    on the distant fields, those are.
Between three and four –
                    and not before! –
We'll get our second wind.
And on the high road a warm dust,
close on forty, will descend.

Kiev
January 1980

14.

Where instead of air there is swearing in buses,
The snore of the barracks instead of a new home...
Oh, native land, why
Have you got me up at such an early hour
Like a sleepy child from its bed?
Have the Tartars been pressing?
But no – not a word!
Darkness and cockroaches alone,
And the Russian spirit.
The geese have flown.

Kiev
January 1980

15.

With a Polish *grosz* on a little chain,
With the aristocratic wind in my pockets
I'll go round the market, the market
Facing the sun today at noon.
I am silent almost without an accent:
I don't ask prices, don't haggle,
Because the sun is watering –
Going to one's head now with a green,
and now with a lilac ringing,
Like a performing bear, moving
Round the circle, collecting Polish *groszy*.
So I'll throw my *grosz* in the hat,
The monkey will pull out my fortune –
And I'll cast it to the winds,
Without reading it.
For what can I do with it,
Since it's in Cyrillic letters – my fortune?
Except set it free...
Oh, if only it would let me go!

Kiev
April 1980

16.

I know this is hard to believe,
But we all lived –
Although not for long –
We all dug our own canals
And dressed to a strange fashion.
We were young, pointed,
And on our fingernails there were gold spots,
And we were reflected in our canals –
Light-haired, in circles made of haloes –
But our time raised its hackles,
And premonition made our lips grow dumb,
But still we lived.
And your tomorrow
Dawned on us like a deserted morning.
And what did we care about our biographies,
If we were alive?
They'd write them later.

Kiev
April 1980

17.

Are you weeping,
         my missing motherland?
You have scattered your children,
And how will you gather them now?
And indeed where are you yourself,
         in what skies of your territory...
Murdered one,
         why are you weeping again?
Why do you tear your foundlings' souls in the nest,
Why do you groan in a voice
         that brings a tremor to one's lips?
What more is wrong with you, what more trouble are you in now,
Murdered one?
By what cross now
Have you not wept,
On what squares now
Have you not shouted in madness blasphemous words?
You knock on my door
(Oh, I know: those who will knock after
Will not spare)
And croak: 'I'm alive!'

Kiev
April 1980

18.

I still think I see the city where no one lives,
Where the pinkies of the weeds
  have pushed apart the order of the concrete,
And in the debris of the church still young the Madonna
Like a mermaid over a slipper,
    yet waits for Lady Day.
If not today then tomorrow: after all it is summer now forever,
And the trees won't lose the children,
    and they won't feel cold for clothes.
The dragonflies are triumphant,
    the water in the rails has rusted,
Stars that have not been seen before are showing through.
And they're neither to be snatched away by the school bell,
Nor wiped out by December:
Wolf evening and midday of wormwood –
Be consoled, Madonna!
From the grass to the beasts –
    none of us will ever die.
We shall be with you.
This city is already outside the law.

Kiev
February 1981

19.

There on the roof no one weeps,
There the moon arches its back.
There forever the ball has rolled
into a corner behind the ancient eaves.
The sparrows' conversations
Assume the scale of battles.
And the snowy mountains are sad
That they've already done their flying.
And by honest combat the old argument
Is resolved at the cats' drinking-bout:
Does valerian smell of spring
Or do the stairs smell of valerian?

Kiev
February 1982

20.

Let's celebrate the thunderstorm:
In the garden the hysteria of the lilac,
The blind illumination of the window
And on the balcony a dragonfly.
The bouquet in the trembling phial has died,
And from the sky – thunder and fire,
As though a gypsy woman's unsold
Violet balloon had burst!
How accidental are our holidays
And unexpected to us,
With what an extraordinary fate
They're endowed – for the umpteenth time!
And, truly, is it worth being sad
That the telephones have fallen silent,
That winter letters are not brought...
Already Epiphany is over our shoulders.
It's April. We celebrate the thunderstorm.

Kiev,
April 1982

KGB PRISON, KIEV 1982-83

21.

My anguish is a homely beast,
She's quiet and knows the word 'shoo!'.
She doesn't need much: a scratch behind the ear,
To be fed a sweet and the whisper: 'stay!'
She doesn't seize me by the throat
And never thrusts herself when strangers are present.
The simple little song of the minute hand
Will comfort her and charm her.
She will climb onto my knee,
Rub her nose on me in childlike fashion and fall asleep.
And the absurd iron transom
will throw shadows onto my exercise book.
And only at night, like a mouse in straw,
She'll fuss about, and in half-sleep
Quietly begin to whimper about the warm house
That you are still going to build for me.

KGB Prison, Kiev
September 1982

22.

Sweets, who wants sweets!
There are none sweeter, none more transparent!
Come flying quickly, little terrors:
Made of slivers – a whole bouquet!
A yellow hare, a red cockerel,
And four lilac elephants.
Take two at once:
What joy, if it's alone?
The secret of my sweets is:
Wind, mint and barberries.
There are none sweeter, none cooler –
Come flying and take them boldly:
Lick them – in your mouth there's a chill,
Bite them – they melt like a dream,
Look through them – they're green ice,
Yellow honey, a raspberry chime!
Din-don – a pane of sugar!
This summer, in this garden –
Come flying – you're in luck!
Tomorrow I won't come here.
The yellow hare, the lilac elephant
Won't be back – and just as well.
It's an old law of sweets:
What joy, if it's every day?

KGB Prison, Kiev
September 1982

23.

Moments of memory of the unsurvived summer
Came to me and stood outside the door,
Simple and solemn as children,
In the tight costumes of princes and wild animals.
They held their treasures
So carefully in their thin little hands –
All the thunderstorms, all the beetles!
I felt sorry for them.
And we began to talk about poetry.
After that we turned crumpled pages,
After that were silent. And after that
The soundless midnight birds
Crowded outside the only window.
And they looked so attentively,
So steadfastly, as though they were keeping count,
Recalling each day of the week.
And the visitors said goodbye and left.
And in confusion I'm gathering my strength.
Just a little longer! I ought
To have let those birds in long ago.
Their time has come.
But how hard it is for me to open the window!

KGB Prison, Kiev
October 1982

24.

And here's the winter! Who'd like some freshness?
The snow-bound gutter crunches...
Don't let your teeth catch cold! Like a starched
Gown, like holiness and mint –
Close against your lips! Close against your feet!
Catch it! Trample it!
It's all so absurd,
So capsized, laughing,
As though the angels were sprinkling
white breadcrumbs on us –
There are enough for all the prisoners in the world!
In a most generous ration – a fluffy layer:
For all the kids – like sweet cotton-wool,
For all the murdered ones – behind the fence
Like the whitest down;
For me – like spring.

KGB Prison, Kiev
December 1982

Dance with a Shadow

It's the thirty-first – *din-don!*
Close on midnight – sleep begone!
With you I'll go – eye to eye –
Into the New Year's dance!
I'll swing my skirt – of lace!
Send me whirling, falcon – only just alive!
Let the candles all become one,
Let our souls all stand up straight,
Let our misery blow like smoke, out through the window...
Let it be dark to our eyes!
And anyway, I've pencilled my eyes...
And under my heart – that's not a needle,
But an eyelash that's fallen – take it out!
And brush the snow from your head!
And the table is covered with an embroidered cloth,
And the border is all crosses,
And the glasses – chime! – fill them fuller!
Look – there's a fir-needle at the bottom...So drink!
With you I'll take a sip
Of New Year's ice,
I'll pull you
Into the dance – all night long;
This is our night – *din-don!*
And it will come true.
Make a wish on the dream.

KGB Prison, Kiev
31 December 1982

26.

All as I asked:
There will be for me, will be
(O Lord, thank you!)
A far road
And new people.
There will be for me, will be
A homeless song
And a proud memory.
There will be for me a heaven
Won by honour,
And a cloak beneath my feet.
There will be for me –
Sometimes –
A happy story
Made of wormwood and mint,
A dress, a semi-mask,
A lace dance...
And no one will say:
'She saw life and that was it!'

KGB Prison, Kiev
January 1983

LABOUR CAMP 385, BARASHEVO, 1983-85

27.

I don't know how they'll kill me:
Whether they'll shoot me down at the start of the turmoil –
And I will press my confused hands
Against the hole where my heart was.
And they'll sew
Me a white legend, and fit me,
And dress me – later, only, later,
When it's over! When they count the losses,
Heat thoroughly each house that has survived,
And are suddenly confused, as they close the doors,
And grow sad – about whom, no one knows.
And perhaps even earlier – maybe right now:
They will undress me – and throw me into the concrete,
          the stiff cold
ordained by law! Behind the signature of a doctor –
To be a cripple and condemned to death!
So that without hesitation – slowly – I'll go to the bottom!
In accordance with the directions of the regime!
Oh, white legend! Cold!
And – from head to toe – not to be torn away!
Or perhaps, more simply – as news in a letter:
'You know…It's turned out…So what, be brave!
You're strong…' And will I be able to hold back my laughter
At the crumpled sheets of paper? How press myself
Like the hole, where my heart was – just now –
Against my hands – already superfluous and unimportant?
And after that – how? Beyond the brink? Beyond the limit
that can't be overstepped? That's measured off? Made of paper?
Oh, only not that way! Not through you,
My own! Let it not be you, let it be others!
For it's not mercy I want! But another death –
Cement, a bullet! Only not words!
And in any case, what nonsense am I talking? It's not for me
To assume doubt in my friends, in my sweetheart –
To assume panic! With a single 'no'
I sweep aside the assumption of greasepaint
On the most faithful souls of all the earth,
On the most vehement and the most proud!

What, wolf age? Do you turn up your snout to a beast?
Who ought to be afraid of whom – do you know?
Shoot!

ZhKh–385/3-4 Small Zone
15 June 1983

28.

Strawberry Town

In Strawberry Town
There are clear-ringing windows.
In Strawberry Town
There's milk for the cat,
In Strawberry Town
There are gingerbreads with pictures,
Little towers with clocks,
Gypsy women with baskets,
Puddles and ships.
Dates and bananas,
Proud crows,
Wise rams.
Cartoons all evening,
Ice creams all day,
And on Sundays
You can get extra ones!
And already there's been seen
In Strawberry Town
An expression of happiness
On the horse's face!
And there are hedgehogs,
Tigers and bears there, too!
Let's buy a pile of sugar —
And quickly go
To Strawberry Town!

ZhKh–385/3-4 Small Zone
July 1983

29.

O.M.

[*Osip Mandelstam*]

Who left neither son nor home,
Lifted into the blizzard in the midst of a line,
Driven along the chipped road –
By an absurd wafting of the hand,
An immortal birdlike flap –
Have you not
Blessed me for this frozen journey?
And I am not afraid to look
The driver of the black horses in the eye-sockets:
Neither the circling and trembling of strange birds,
Nor the rumbling of the last cloudy limit –
Will succeed in frightening me, once you
Have already come out to the riverbank to greet me,
And you wait by the edge of the murky water.
I recognise your flap – and the links
Of the powerless bonds break, and mortality falls away!
And soon you will walk on the firmament
And will give me your hand, so that oblivion
Does not splash up to my knees.

ZhKh–385/3-4 Small Zone
August 1983

30.

If you come out of the evening straight into the grass,
Along the cracks in the asphalt – into the twilight of the plants,
Then tomorrow it will come true – and when you're awake
– the fabulous summer of happy portents.
All the signs are for rain,
All the rain is for the crops,
And all the postmen have good news.
All the grasshoppers must sing,
And creators must perish
From love for those they have created – as beautiful as songs.
And then, and then –
the scales will fall from our eyes,
And with enraptured vision – different from before –
We shall read the letters that did not arrive,
And completely
Justify the hopes of friends who did not survive.
And we shall raise from the ash
Our joyful house,
So that it may stand inspired and steadfast.
How happy we shall be – some day later on!
How we need to survive!
Well, if not ourselves – then our sweethearts.

ZhKh–385/3-4 Small Zone
3 October 1983

31.

Give me a nickname, prison,
In this first April,
On this evening of sadness,
Shared with you.
In this hour of your songs
About evil and good,
Your confessions of love,
And spicy jokes.
From me they have taken
My friends and my folk,
Torn my cross from its chain
And removed my clothes,
And then with their boots
Kicked me senseless,
Beating out with prejudice
The remnants of hope.
My name has been filed,
Both profile and front –
In a numbered dossier,
In the custody of the law –
Not mine at all!
The same as you –
No one, nothing!
On the window bars –
Here I am, all of me – nickname me,
Give me a name, prison,
See off to deportation
Not an urchin, but a *zek*,
So I may be greeted
More warmly by Kolyma,
The place of the exiles and executions
Of the twentieth century.

ZhKh–385/3-4 Small Zone
5 October 1983

32.

What do you remember of us, my sad one,
As you send me weightless dreams?
What do you rave about in the empty nights,
When the walls are cramped to one's breathing?
Do you remember the first meetings,
The distant camp, the crossroads of the ages?
Does the blue pulsation of your temples
Speak with an unknown discourse?
Do you remember the wild herd of barbarians,
And on the crest of the last wall
Do we – the last ones – hold off the siege,
And are we struck down by the same arrow?
Do you remember the daring escape at dawn,
The inspired shivering of the fugitives,
And the curly east wind
Throwing showers in my face?
I don't remember if there was a chase,
But no doubt it fell far behind,
And the merry sea horses
Carried us to a warm land.
Do you remember the strange blue dress –
And the child fell quiet under the shawl...
In that year the curse was fulfilled,
And to someone they shouted: 'We're brothers!'
And someone was raised on a bayonet...
How then we lost each other –
In the turmoil, in the dust of the road –
And did not know if it was for a day or forever?
And – are you aware of it – found each other again?
Through death, through the years and the years,
Through the features of new births,
Through the dark waters of oblivion,
Through the cell-bars I whisper: it's you!

ZhKh–385/3-4 Small Zone
8 October 1983

33.

Here's December once again
Spreading out canvases,
And the roadways are full
Of a patterned crackling,
And in vain the four
Elements bustle
To preserve us from his
Deadly purity.
Let's launch our planets
Along former circles –
Probably the road will turn out
White for us.
The snows will lick
Our lifelines clean –
But it still remains for us
To go through the epilogue.
But, leaving the seal
Of stubborn footprints,
To climb the frozen steps
To the executioner's block –
And to feel the stern coldness
Of a clean shirt
Like grace
On weak shoulders.

ZhKh–385/3-4 Small Zone
December 1983

34.

Tanya Osipova, how sick of you I am!
Even here – the two of us: the twinlike effect is to blame!
The grey wind is taking a walk round our plank bed,
And the mice have come out for a promenade.
We're in SHIZO again, oh, they don't pat our backs!
Beneath a single star to freeze away from all cares.
Well, if the worst comes to the worst – you in SHIZO, and I
        on hunger-strike.
Or the same, but the other way round.
It's clear that our angels have found the time and the place
To remember: where we hung about separately, and they're right.
Where were you in Moscow at the time of my flying visits?
And where was I when you were in Lefortovo?
How could two such feeble-voiced ones not sing the same song?
You won't escape fate: since ours haven't brought us together –
The authorities have done us a bad turn, and now there's
        nothing for it!
They've brought the skillet; take some for us both.

ZhKh–385/2 SHIZO
30 January 1984

55

35.

We won't go into one and the same river,
Won't move apart the overgrown banks,
For us there'll be no lame man
Who's ready to ferry us across.

There'll be an evening – warm as an infusion
Of dark herbs: indolence and silence.
Then they will retreat, the camp bunk,
The cold of the cell, the wind from the window.

But we'll remember conversations in a circle,
The happiest dreams in semi-delirium,
The Mordvin women shoving a crust:
'Take some bread, don't go hungry!'

And this is for us to take to our sweethearts,
Confiding in honest fashion – to each something:
All the terrible things – to ourselves,
All the evil things – past him,
All Earth's kindness – into his shoulder.

ZhKh–385/3-4 Small Zone
16 February 1984

36.

Lilies and raspberries,
ermines, white dogs,
And banners with the sweep of lions,
And patterned merlons.
Over the planking thunder the hooves,
The burnished steel is warm.
And a curly scroll flies down
From a hewn table.
While from the heavens come portents and fish,
Someone's wings and voices.
Boulders tower into cathedrals,
But the prophets have withdrawn to the forests.
The imprints of Judas's hands
Are on the coins – not in hearts.
But poisoned gloves
Are given to little girls in the palaces.

ZhKh – 385/3-4 Small Zone
12 April 1984

37.

I'll buy a big trunk
And pack everything in there:
The picture of the sinner in hell
And the sleepy tom-cat.
And the maps of countries that don't exist,
And the bowler hat,
And also the old pistol,
The catapult and the whistle.
And with this same catapult
Tomorrow I'll be on my way,
And – in one place on horseback, in another on foot –
I'll get somewhere.
Even though the land to which I'll come
Has been obliterated on the crease of the map!
With the picture of the sinner in hell
We'll light a camp-fire.
The tom-cat will scare away all the wild animals
That look out of the bushes,
But the sugar will make kinder
The tailed and tailless.
We'll brew the tea in the kettle,
And with it a fallen leaf.
All who are near and far
Will come to us at the sound of the whistle.
We'll sing songs,
Chatter about this and that,
And no one, no one, no one
Will chase us off to bed!
And the stars will rise above our heads
More brightly than sweets...
And in order not to spoil it all with an ending,
I won't go back home!

ZhKh–385/2 PKT
28 July 1984

Well, let's live
The way our souls allow,
Not asking any other sustenance.
I'll buy myself a pet mouse,
A dog is impossible yet.
And he and I will live and get on,
And read letters in the corner.
And he will get into my bed
Without having washed the ash from his paws.
And if letters suddenly don't arrive –
(After all, anything can happen on the way!) –
There he'll be, little grey one,
Angrily twirling his nose.
And then he'll bury himself in my palm:
'Remember.' he'll say, 'that there are two of us!
Well, we needn't both drink validol,
Let's chew a bit of bread instead!'
I'll unwrap the crushed heel,
And we'll look more kindly on the world,
And he and I will dream up the kind of land
In which there are no cats or camps.
In no time at all we'll abolish the cold there,
Grow bananas in the gardens...
Perhaps after our term they'll send us there,
But more likely it will be Magadan.
But, when they take me to the halting place
And lead me through the search –
He'll follow at my heels behind me,
And he'll get everywhere.
I'll put him in a secret pocket,
So he gets warm while the wheels rumble.
And honourably we'll divide the sugar that we eat –
Ten grammes each.
And no matter where our route lies –
Where we are is nothing to us now.
For we're both old *zeks* – I
and my long-tailed creature.

Behind any bars will be home to us,
Behind any February – spring...
And we'll get a dog, too,
But in better times.

ZhKh–385/2 PKT
8 August 1984

39.

They've learned, I suppose, to roll up time into conserves,
And mixed condensed night into every age.
This century grows ever darker,
And the twenty-first will not come quickly
To wipe the names from yesterday's prison wall.

We have laden it with the voices of departed friends,
The names of unborn children – for a new wall.
We've equipped it with such love, but we ourselves
Are not its oarsmen, have not even been called on board.

But covering the measured load with coarse bast matting,
We will still manage to sift the grain by handfuls –
So we cover our palms with wounds, but select the dragons' teeth
From the sowing that is destined to rise after us.

ZhKh–385/2 SHIZO
November 1984

40.

Our firmament's rather solid –
Like the cold of a glass retort.
Our world is eternal enough –
We'll both perish sooner than it does.
But all the same we write letters
In deserted Novembers.
Didn't you know, Creator –
Homunculi are stubborn folk!
And will produce stubborn folk,
Ashamed to hunch their shoulders,
Able with God's gaze
To cross human eyes!
So is it strange, Creator,
That in the course of the experiment
There's not enough for everyone of the humility
That's been supplied for mortals?
To each other we'll – tear!
(Oh, mind the apparatus!)
To all Your labyrinths –
Inventing gunpowder!
To our mortal agony –
Forming the words of victory,
To pain – biting back a smile,
Without a moan – after Whom would we moan?
Is it not Your law that clay
Is only stronger after firing?
What if the united two
Cannot be dissolved by means of a tube?
Into the glimmering retort
Look closely and shrug your shoulders:
Well, what is to to You – of the whole flock,
Two have strayed again!
...It's time to turn off the switch.
So why do You delay, Father?
What else can be brought down
On us, apart from eternal night?

What other behest do You
Appoint to your proud ones?
...We stand, throwing back our faces
Into the unswitched-off light.

ZhKh–385/3-4 Small Zone
January 1985

41.

If you can't sleep – count up to a hundred,
And drive these thoughts away.
I know: I can't be reached now
And can't be helped in any way.
So don't tear, as you burn in a night fever,
The white bandage of your last sleep!
Perhaps I will soon come back again –
And then you will recognise me.
I'll be a child or a bush –
With hands more tender there are none,
And you must invent a story for me
With a happy ending – and true.
I will be grass or sand –
So I'll be warmer to embrace,
But if I'm a hungry dog –
You must feed me.
Like a gypsy woman I'll catch at your sleeve,
Or hurl myself at your window like a bird –
But don't chase me away when you recognise me.
For I'll only have come – to take a look.
And one day in snow, or perhaps in rain
You'll come across a frozen kitten –
And again it will be me.
And you will be granted the power to save
Anyone you like, in whatever trouble.
But by that time I will be everywhere,
Everywhere on your path.

ZhKh–385/2 PKT
October 1985

THE WEST:
FROM 1987

42.

You and I are transparent as shadows,
Because it's a special evening:
Whether it's because the stars have turned out lucky,
Or whether the smells have hit it off together.
Even the timid fingers of the plants
Greet us so trustingly:
'Today we're as threadbare as the air –
They haven't crushed even our pinkies.'
If you like we can go for a walk along the bay –
A springy film of water –
If you like we can play with the squirrels,
If you like we can comb the wind's withers.
The blossoms on the plum trees are stirring
Like babies in white diapers,
The damp grass is crawling about
And a cricket has begun to chatter in the darkness.
If you like we can answer him in the same way,
Or cry like night birds,
If you like we can hurl ourselves straight into the sky,
As into a pond – and spill the stars.
How the unsaddled wind is trembling!
They're waiting for us there, we're not dreaming that.
What do we know of fact and fable?
Look – a raven. Don't be afraid – it's a prophetic one.

Chicago
26 April 1987

43.

In Italy the clouds are baroque,
And the Tiber lies down in taut loops,
While from the convex hills the birds fly down,
And every arc is divinely weightless.
Whence are known to me in advance
The path half wiped away by the rains,
The grassblade sprouted on the sundial
And such an unhurried passage of time,
As though ahead were all those ages
That have cut roads into this earth.
And it's too early to talk about an epilogue,
When every line throbs so
And wants to live...
In the mountains the gods are laughing.
And death does not see us from afar.

Rome
28 August 1987

44.

The cypresses, like horses, sleep standing up,
The blue light is given its freedom,
And the soul is given peace, for all times:
Today, or a hundred deaths ago.
We fed the clouds of the heavens from our hands,
Our lips burned over a subterranean flame,
The seas carried us and the forest hid us,
The dust of the road gave us warmth,
The South showered us with nocturnal stars,
The North spread at our feet the ermine of the snows –
And no one believed they would kill us:
Not one of all our friends and enemies.
The wings of victory crossed us with white,
Red the lost battle flowed into the grasses.
But again and again descends to us the light
That is far above earthly cares – blue.

Seriati
1 September 1987

45.

Drawing near, September has hung the stars lower –
And in gales fish splash to them with their fins.
At night the callous waves grind stone,
And the houses of the shores hide and silently listen.

A petal of space has curled up and lain down like the bay,
The hills have risen like dogs, with quietly bristling hides.
A man sits drawing shapes in the sand.
In a couple of thousand years he'll find out how to be happy.

Riva Trigoso
27 September 1987

46.

Letter Home

There are countries in the world that the eyes suck in,
There are lands beautiful to the point of sadness!
And the evening mountains – for every voice,
And open to all the autostrada's speeds.
Sweet is the apple smell of other languages,
And trusting are the rivers where the trout dance.
Far, far away
From our kin and our enemies
Friends have kept us warm in un-Russian houses.
The foreign earth is kind to us, but it is not for us to lie in it:
Another fate has been nailed to our palms.
And again we lace up
Our shoes for the road,
Even though we know there won't be any more pursuit.
Only how can we forget our land in its need,
Since they crossed us in Russian style when they saw us off?
One day we will say
At the Last Judgement
That we have fulfilled all that we vowed at the station.
From another place of arms we're still in the same battle,
Here we'll bloody our lips on the same freedom!
Even though it isn't we who measure out our road –
God grant that we get there –
From sunset to sunrise.

Milan
28 September 1987

47.

Rejoice, my wild falcon:
The day is given to us for hunting,
Rejoice, my wild horse:
Forget about the bridle.
Over the June hills
We'll rush in flight at a gallop,
And towards evening the Lord
Will light a great star for us.
To those who have sheltered us for the night
We'll give generously of our prey,
To the girl who woke us
We shall give a resonant ring...
Smile, my joy,
When you hear the falcons shrieking!
If you give birth to a son –
Let me know by the first messenger.

Newcastle upon Tyne
9 June 1988

48.

For the blessed cries of the cicada,
For the stubbornness of roasted flints –
Our souls will return to Hellas
For a farewell circle over it.

At the end of the torn thread
Having given breathing and weight to the clay,
All the forests and rocky mountain ridges
We'll see from the hot skies.

And then we'll laugh happily,
And the coachman will whip up the horses.
An olive tree will carelessly splash
An overwound branch to us before the wind.

Skiatos
28 August 1988

49.

The Blackened Kettle

So you lived, cheerfully getting old,
Warming your hands on a blackened kettle,
Brighter than all the market sweets –
The insolent riff-raff of homeless sages
In tinsel and lace rags,
In the smells of a travelling menagerie –
By evening – unrecognised princes,
At nights – 'How could you ever want go with me?'
Tomorrow the white raven will begin to laugh,
A new town will show you
With the hubbub of children from whose well
To water your tired horses.
You'll travel on.
The posters will fade.
The little terrors who raved about you
Will make their way in life. Your bells
Won't change the world. Hush...hush.

                    *

Little girl, how could you ever want to go with me?
The ribs of the show-booth are falling.
Our women grow old prematurely.
Not one is happy. Not one.
Don't look at the embroidered shawls
And the spangles of the sweaty saddle!
Our women have been so much wronged
That their smiles are like tar
That has seethed into their mouths. Their cheeks
Are eaten away by rouge, their breasts by children.
I'm deserting you – without deceit.
I'll bear the slap. Forget it.

                    *

If it is anywhere, God's paradise,
My old parrot will be there now,
Who told the fortunes of half Europe,
Insulted all the worldly powers
With his cursing in countless languages,
Took his last gasp in my arms,
Not feeling sorry for anyone any more:
I was the only one he called a fool.

Paris
6 May 1989

50.

We're still living in that poor year
Where there's a smell of carbolic acid, as in a kindergarten,
Where the paint's been licked from the toys long ago,
But where tomorrow we're promised the cinema,
Where we are slowly taught our ABC:
To sing and dance and not rely on tears.
But where in the evening now one, now another
As though by chance – by the leaf of the door,
And with quiet despair – says:
'No. Not for me.'

28 July 1990

51.

The trees did not pluck the apple
And are not ashamed of their nakedness.
And send naive leaves
To those who are down there, in the semi-basement:
'I see a cloud.
And you?'

King's Lynn
20 September 1990

AUTHORS PUBLISHED BY
BLOODAXE BOOKS

FLEUR ADCOCK
GÖSTA ÅGREN
ANNA AKHMATOVA
SIMON ARMITAGE
NEIL ASTLEY
ATTILA THE STOCKBROKER
ANNEMARIE AUSTIN
SHIRLEY BAKER
GEREME BARMÉ
MARTIN BELL
CONNIE BENSLEY
STEPHEN BERG
YVES BONNEFOY
MARTIN BOOTH
KAMAU BRATHWAITE
GORDON BROWN
BASIL BUNTING
CIARAN CARSON
ANGELA CARTER
JOHN CASSIDY
JAROSLAV CEJKA
MICHAL CERNÍK
AIMÉ CÉSAIRE
SID CHAPLIN
RENÉ CHAR
GEORGE CHARLTON
EILÉAN NÍ CHUILLEANÁIN
KILLARNEY CLARY
BRENDAN CLEARY
JACK CLEMO
HARRY CLIFTON
JACK COMMON
STEWART CONN
NOEL CONNOR
DAVID CONSTANTINE
CHARLOTTE CORY
JENI COUZYN
HART CRANE
ADAM CZERNIAWSKI
PETER DIDSBURY
STEPHEN DOBYNS
MAURA DOOLEY
KATIE DONOVAN
JOHN DREW
IAN DUHIG
HELEN DUNMORE
DOUGLAS DUNN
STEPHEN DUNSTAN
JACQUES DUPIN
G.F. DUTTON
LAURIS EDMOND
ALISTAIR ELLIOT
STEVE ELLIS
ODYSSEUS ELYTIS
EURIPIDES
DAVID FERRY

EVA FIGES
SYLVA FISCHEROVÁ
TONY FLYNN
VICTORIA FORDE
TUA FORSSTRÖM
JIMMY FORSYTH
LINDA FRANCE
ELIZABETH GARRETT
ARTHUR GIBSON
PAMELA GILLILAN
ANDREW GREIG
JOHN GREENING
PHILIP GROSS
JOSEF HANZLÍK
TONY HARRISON
ANNE HÉBERT
HAROLD HESLOP
DOROTHY HEWETT
SELIMA HILL
FRIEDRICH HÖLDERLIN
MIROSLAV HOLUB
FRANCES HOROVITZ
DOUGLAS HOUSTON
JOHN HUGHES
PAUL HYLAND
KATHLEEN JAMIE
VLADIMÍR JANOVIC
B.S. JOHNSON
LINTON KWESI JOHNSON
JOOLZ
JENNY JOSEPH
SYLVIA KANTARIS
JACKIE KAY
BRENDAN KENNELLY
SIRKKA-LIISA KONTTINEN
JEAN HANFF KORELITZ
DENISE LEVERTOV
HERBERT LOMAS
MARION LOMAX
EDNA LONGLEY
FEDERICO GARCÍA LORCA
GEORGE MacBETH
PETER McDONALD
DAVID McDUFF
MEDBH McGUCKIAN
MAIRI MacINNES
CHRISTINE McNEILL
OSIP MANDELSTAM
GERALD MANGAN
E.A. MARKHAM
WILLIAM MARTIN
JILL MAUGHAN
GLYN MAXWELL
HENRI MICHAUX
JOHN MINFORD
ADRIAN MITCHELL

JOHN MONTAGUE
EUGENIO MONTALE
DAVID MORLEY
RICHARD MURPHY
BILL NAUGHTON
SEAN O'BRIEN
JULIE O'CALLAGHAN
JOHN OLDHAM
MICHEAL O'SIADHAIL
TOM PAULIN
GYÖRGY PETRI
TOM PICKARD
JILL PIRRIE
SIMON RAE
DEBORAH RANDALL
IRINA RATUSHINSKAYA
MARIA RAZUMOVSKY
JEREMY REED
PETER REDGROVE
ANNE ROUSE
CAROL RUMENS
LAWRENCE SAIL
EVA SALZMAN
SAPPHO
WILLIAM SCAMMELL
DAVID SCOTT
JO SHAPCOTT
SIR ROY SHAW
JAMES SIMMONS
MATT SIMPSON
LEMN SISSAY
DAVE SMITH
KEN SMITH
SEAN SMITH
STEPHEN SMITH
EDITH SÖDERGRAN
PIOTR SOMMER
MARIN SORESCU
LEOPOLD STAFF
PAULINE STAINER
EIRA STENBERG
MARTIN STOKES
KAREL SYS
RABINDRANATH TAGORE
JEAN TARDIEU
D.M. THOMAS
R.S. THOMAS
TOMAS TRANSTRÖMER
MARINA TSVETAYEVA
FRED VOSS
ALAN WEARNE
NIGEL WELLS
C.K. WILLIAMS
JOHN HARTLEY WILLIAMS
JAMES WRIGHT
BENJAMIN ZEPHANIAH

For a complete catalogue of books published by Bloodaxe, pleaee write to:
Bloodaxe Books Ltd, P.O. Box 1SN, Newcastle upon Tyne NE99 1SN.